An Eskimo Family

This edition published 1985 by Lerner Publications Company.
All U.S. rights reserved. No part of this book may be reproduced
in any form whatsoever without permission in writing from the
publisher except for the inclusion of brief quotations in an
acknowledged review. ©1979 by Bryan and Cherry Alexander.
First published by A & C Black (Publishers) Limited, London,
under the title *Eskimo Boy*.

LIBRARY OF CONGRESS CATALOGING IN PUBLICATION DATA

Alexander, Bryan.
　An Eskimo family.

　Originally published: Eskimo boy. London: A & C
Black, ©1979.
　Summary: Describes the life of a fifteen-year-old
Eskimo boy and his family who live in the world's most
northern village, Siorapaluk, Greenland.
　1. Eskimos—Greenland—Juvenile literature.
[1. Greenland—Social life and customs. 2. Eskimos—
Greenland] I. Alexander, Cherry. II. Title.
E99.E7A487　1985　　　998.2　　　84-19475
ISBN 0-8225-1656-X (lib. bdg.)

Manufactured in the United States of America

　　3　4　5　6　7　8　9　10　94　93　92　91　90　89

An Eskimo Family

Bryan and Cherry Alexander

Lerner Publications Company · Minneapolis

Otto Simigak (si-mi-ak) is an Eskimo. He is 15 years old and lives with his parents in Greenland. His father is a hunter, and Otto often hunts with him.

Otto and his parents live in the world's most northern village, Siorapaluk (hiora-pal-ook), which means "little sandy beach" in Greenlandic. There *is* a sandy beach there, but you can only see it for a few weeks in the summer. The rest of the year it is covered with snow and ice. Siorapaluk is very small, and only seventy Eskimos live there.

Otto's family has a wooden house in the center of the village. The house has two rooms. The family sleeps in the small room and uses the larger one as a living room and kitchen. Since there is no gas or electricity in the village, they use a coal stove to keep their house warm.

Before they had wooden houses, Eskimos lived in small huts made of sod. The walls were lined with sealskin, and oil lamps provided warmth and light.

No one in Siorapaluk lives in an igloo. Sometimes, though, when they are out hunting, Eskimos build igloos as shelter from a storm.

Because Otto's home is close to the North Pole, it gets very cold in the winter. The temperature drops as low as −40°C (−40°F). Even the sea freezes. As soon as the sea ice is thick enough, the Eskimos travel on it with sleds pulled by huskies.

To get enough food for themselves and their dogs, Otto and his father go hunting whenever they can. They usually hunt mammals that live in the sea—walrus, seals, polar bears, and whales.

During the winter, hunting is especially hard. Each year the sun sets in October and is not seen again until the next February. It is dark all day and all night.

To breathe, the seals and walrus make holes in the sea ice. The hunters must find these breathing holes by listening for them.

When a hunter finds a seal's breathing hole, he waits quietly by it. He may have to stand very still for an hour or more before he has a chance to harpoon the seal.

The Eskimos also try to catch seals during the winter by setting nets underneath the ice. On nice days, Otto and his father travel out onto the ice by dog sled to check their seal nets. They don't always catch a seal, but Otto's father is teaching him the best places to set his nets.

During the long winter months, Otto and his father spend a lot of time at home. They make harpoons, repair dog harnesses, fix their nets, and take care of other odd jobs.

Otto's father, Kaugunak (cow-oo-nak), likes to carve figures in soapstone and ivory. He sells them at the trading post. Otto's mother, Nivikanguak (nivi-king-oo-ak), is always busy. She makes fur clothes for the family from the skins of the seals that Otto and his father have caught.

Siorapaluk does not have running water. Each day Otto drives his dog sled out to collect chunks of ice from nearby icebergs. The family melts the ice in a big pot on their stove and uses the water for drinking and washing. Otto and his friends also collect ice for the old people in the village.

Since there is no television in Siorapaluk, the people must make their own entertainment. They visit each other's houses to drink tea and talk. Otto likes to visit Imina, an old man who tells Otto tales from long ago—stories about monsters that lived in the ice cap and about the first white men who visited the land.

Each year on February 17, everyone climbs the mountain behind the village to watch the sun rise for the first time that year. On the evening of the first sunrise, a party is held in the village hall. Children play games, including the Eskimo version of tug-of-war shown here.

On the first day the sun is only above the horizon for a few minutes before it sets again. From then on it will stay up a little longer each day. By May, the sun is shining all day and all night.

The weather warms up more slowly. February and March are still the coldest months of the year. There are often bad storms which last for several days.

Otto and Kaugunak know the dangers of arctic storms and how easily they can freeze people to death. They stay indoors and wait for the howling wind to stop. But even in the coldest weather, their huskies stay outside.

During the summer when it's warm, Otto wears jeans and other modern clothes. These are bought at the trading post. But during the winter he wears fur clothes because they are warmer.

When Otto and his father go out hunting, they wear *kamik*, or sealskin boots, with socks made from the fur of the arctic hare. Their pants are made from polar bear skin, and their hooded parkas are made from reindeer skin. Sealskin mittens keep their fingers from frostbite.

March is a good time to hunt walrus in Siorapaluk. The walrus can be found out on the newly formed sea ice where the ice is thin and there are plenty of clams to eat.

It does not take Otto and his father long to prepare for a hunting trip. First they visit the trading post for supplies of tea, sugar, and ammunition. Then they tie everything securely onto their sleds with ropes, hitch up the dogs, and take off.

Because it is so cold, the hunters usually stop every three hours for a mug of hot tea. They make the tea by melting snow in a pan on their small oil-burning stove.

It usually takes the hunters about five hours to reach the new ice where they will find the walrus. The ice is only a few inches thick and bends under their weight. Taking only what they need for the hunt, they walk in single file.

Some days they must walk for many hours while they search for walrus. If they pass an iceberg, one of the hunters will usually climb it to get a better view. When a hunter sees a walrus at its breathing hole, he creeps up very quietly without being noticed. As soon as he is close enough, he throws his harpoon at the walrus.

Walrus are big and very heavy, so it takes several men to haul the dead walrus out of the water. Once they have pulled it onto the ice, the hunters cut it up. The man who threw the harpoon gets the best parts, but all of the hunters get something.

When it begins to get dark, the Eskimos stop hunting. Otto and his father look for a safe piece of ice to camp on. They put up a tent over their sleds and tie it securely to the ice.

Although Otto and his father are hungry and tired after a long day of hunting, they always feed their huskies first.

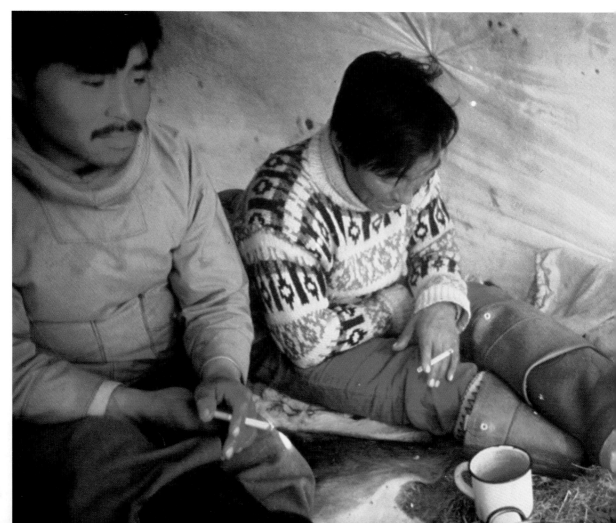

Once the dogs have settled down for the night, Otto and his father go into their tent. They warm themselves next to the stove and hang up their boots to dry. Soon they have a pan of walrus meat cooking and the smell fills the tent.

After they have eaten, they often sit and talk. Kaugunak tells Otto hunting stories from the old days.

As the evening passes, the warmth of the tent and their full stomachs make Otto and Kaugunak sleepy. They sleep on reindeer skins which they have spread over their sleds. The stove they used for cooking burns all night to keep the tent warm.

As long as the weather stays nice, Otto and his father continue to hunt until they have caught enough food. Then, with their sleds heavy with meat, they set off across the ice for home.

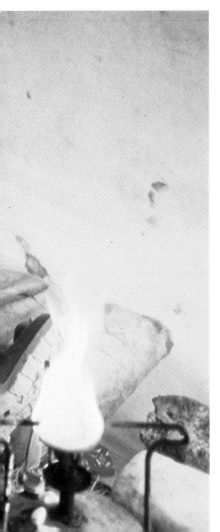

Nivikanguak is always happy to see Otto and Kaugunak come home safely. The new ice can be very dangerous, and some hunters have drifted out to sea when the ice broke around them.

After a long hunting trip, Otto and Kaugunak rest. Otto listens to the radio or plays music on his cassette player. He also likes to go to the films that are shown every week at the village hall. The projector is run by a generator.

By the end of April it is light all night. The weather gradually warms up, and the seals pull themselves up onto the sea ice to sleep in the spring sunshine. It takes great skill to hunt these seals. Because the ice is flat, the seals can easily see someone approach. The hunter has to hide behind a white cloth screen mounted on skis.

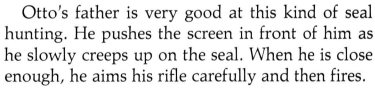

Otto's father is very good at this kind of seal hunting. He pushes the screen in front of him as he slowly creeps up on the seal. When he is close enough, he aims his rifle carefully and then fires.

Nivikanguak cleans the skins they have caught. First she scrapes off the fat with a special knife called a *ulo*. Then she washes the skin several times to get rid of the grease and stretches it out on a frame to dry. She keeps some of the skins to make new clothes and sells the rest at the trading post.

It is too cold in Greenland to farm or grow vegetables, so the Eskimos live on the meat they catch. They eat seal and walrus meat the most often, but they also eat polar bear, whale, arctic hare, fish, and some sea birds. They usually boil their food, but eat some meats dried or raw.

Siorapaluk is a silent place during the winter. The only birds that can survive the long harsh winter are the raven and the ptarmigan, a bird with feathered feet. Each fall the rest of the birds fly south and don't return until the following spring.

Otto and his family always look forward to May, when thousands of auks come to nest near their village. Auks are small birds and are a favorite food of many Eskimos.

As soon as the birds arrive, the family packs a tent and some supplies and sets off into the hills to catch them. The Eskimos hide behind a large rock and scoop the birds out of the sky with a net. It is not easy because the birds fly so fast.

On the hill behind Siorapaluk is a small wooden church. Every Sunday a service is held there. During the week the church is used as a school. All the children between 7 and 12 years old go to class there. After school they play in the snow.

Otto attended school in Siorapaluk until he was 12. Then he went to a boarding school at Thule, about 50 miles (80 kilometers) away. He didn't like it, and when he was 14 he left to become a hunter.

His father was pleased because many of the young men today don't want to become hunters. They want a different kind of life and choose instead to become carpenters or work at the trading post.

Thule is the largest town in the district and has 300 people. Otto and his family go to Thule to visit friends and to shop. They also go there to see the doctor and the dentist.

The trip usually takes them about seven hours by dog sled, but it depends on the condition of the ice. Sometimes they meet a family traveling the other way, and they stop to give the dogs a rest and exchange news.

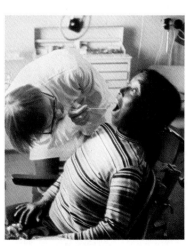

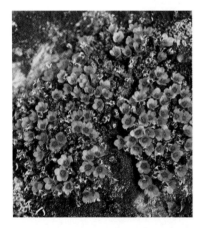

School is over at the end of May and does not begin again until August. Many of the families leave the village to live at camps where the hunting is good. The children love summer. Because it is light all the time, they can play outside longer.

In early June, the sun is very strong and reflects brightly off the ice. The Eskimos have to wear sunglasses or else the snow would blind them. Before they could buy sunglasses, Eskimos used to wear goggles made from bone with two narrow slits to see through.

The warmer weather helps to melt the sea ice. The ice nearest the land is the thickest, and so it is the last to go. Soon the snow on the land also begins to melt. Then, for just a few weeks, the land is covered with millions of beautiful, colorful arctic flowers.

It is too dangerous to drive a dog sled over the sea ice while it is melting. The Eskimos must wait for the ice to disappear completely before they can begin their summer hunting from kayaks and boats. There is usually a big storm that breaks up the ice and blows it all out to sea.

23

When all the ice is gone, Otto and his father travel in their boat to the end of one of the neighboring fjords, or inlets, to hunt narwhals. A narwhal is a small whale about five feet long.

Every summer hundreds of narwhals come into the fjords near Siorapaluk to feed on halibut, polar cod, and other fish. Otto and his father usually camp on a small island where his father has caught many narwhals in the past.

No one knows when the whales will arrive. Sometimes the hunters must wait for several days. Then suddenly someone will shout "Kilalugak!" (crey-la-loo-ak) and all the Eskimos will hurry into their kayaks. As the whales get closer, the hunters can hear them breathing and calling to one another.

If a narwhal surfaces near one of the kayaks, the hunter will paddle very quickly after it and throw his harpoon. A line is attached to the harpoon, and on the other end of the line is a sealskin float that the hunter carries on the back of his kayak. If the harpoon hits the narwhal, the hunter quickly throws the float into the water. The narwhal dives and drags the float down with it. The next time the hunters see the float, they know that the whale is nearby. As the whale surfaces, they kill it with a spear.

When the narwhal is dead, the hunters tow the heavy whale back to their camp. They cut it up and divide it into shares. Although a narwhal is very big, nothing is wasted.

At the end of July the first ship of the year arrives at Thule. It brings supplies for the next twelve months. Otto looks forward to the ship's arrival because it also carries fresh fruit and ice cream.

During August the sun gradually begins to get lower in the sky and the days become shorter. The birds leave their nests and join together in noisy flocks. Soon they will begin their long trip south for the winter.

By mid-September, the summer is over. The temperature once again drops below zero and the first thin blanket of snow settles on the land. Otto and his father make the most of these fall days by hunting seals from their boat. New ice will soon be forming in the fjord.

As winter approaches, the days become shorter and darker. On October 26, Otto and his family have their last glimpse of the sun for four months.

Where Eskimos Live Today

North Pole

U.S.S.R.

ICELAND

East Greenland
Eskimos

GREENLAND

Siberian
Eskimos

Polar
Eskimos

North Alaskan
Eskimos

West Greenland
Eskimos

Igloolik
Eskimos

Baffinland
Eskimos

Southwestern
Alaskan Eskimos

ALASKA
(U.S.)

MacKenzie
Eskimos

Copper
Eskimos

Netsilik
Eskimos

Labrador Coast
Eskimos

Pacific
Eskimos

Sadlirmuit
Eskimos

Caribou
Eskimos

Labrador
Eskimos

CANADA

Eskimos

UNITED STATES

Facts about Eskimos

Otto and his family are Polar Eskimos. Polar Eskimos are one of three different groups of Eskimos living in Greenland. The other groups are East Greenland Eskimos and West Greenland Eskimos.

Eskimos live in three other countries besides Greenland. There are nine different Eskimo groups in Canada, four groups in Alaska, and one group in Russia. In all, there are about 110,000 Eskimo people in the world today.

Most Eskimos live in the same area that their ancestors have always lived in. Many now live in towns with modern houses. They wear modern clothes and eat food bought at the store. Others, like Otto's family, still continue the traditional life of their ancestors.

All Eskimo groups speak the same language but each group has a different dialect, or variation of the language. Eskimos call themselves *Inuit* or *Yuit*. Both words mean "people."

Eskimos

NORTH AMERICA

SOUTH AMERICA

EUROPE

A S I A

AFRICA

AUSTRALIA

Families the World Over

Some children in foreign countries live like you do. Others live very differently. In these books, you can meet children from all over the world. You'll learn about their games and schools, their families and friends, and what it's like to grow up in a faraway land.

Lerner Publications Company, 241 First Avenue North, Minneapolis, Minnesota 55401